Everyone I Love is a Stranger to Someone

☙

Poems by Annelyse Gelman

Write Bloody Publishing
America's Independent Press

Austin, TX

WRITEBLOODY.COM

Everyone I Love is a Stranger to Someone
© 2014 Annelyse Gelman
No part of this book may be used or performed without written consent from the author, except for critical articles or reviews.

Write Bloody
First Edition
ISBN: 978-1938912429

Cover art by Lily Lin
Proofread by Kelly Frances Porter
Bee Illustrations by Annelyse Gelman
Additional Illustrations by Auden Lincoln-Vogel
Edited by Derrick Brown, Brian S. Ellis, Sabrina Swerdloff, and Eliana Gray
Interior layout by Ashley Siebels

Type set in Bergamo from www.theleagueofmoveabletype.com

Printed in Tennessee, USA

Write Bloody Publishing
Austin, TX
Support Independent Presses
writebloody.com

To contact the author, send an email to writebloody@gmail.com

MADE IN THE USA

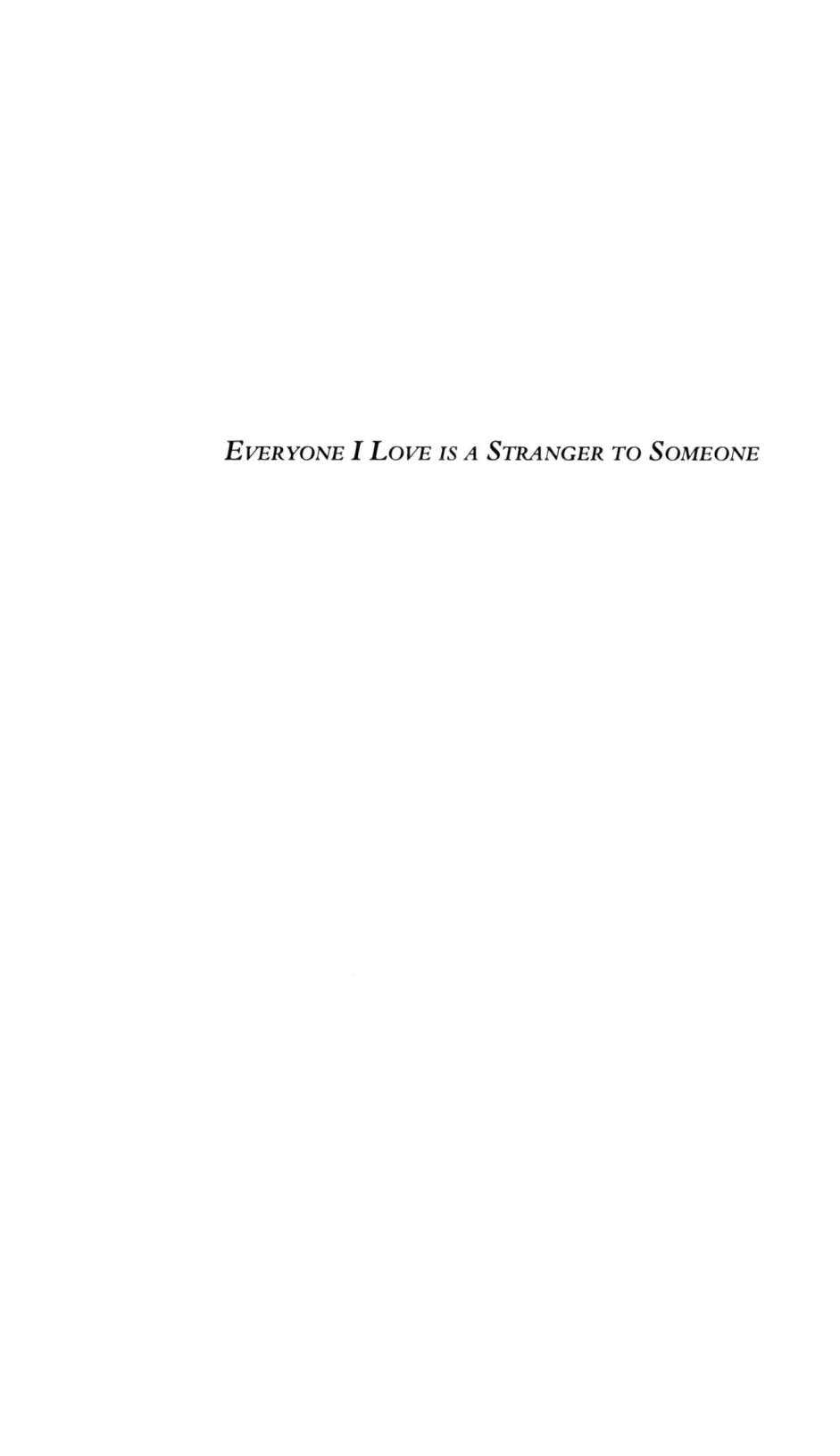

EVERYONE I LOVE IS A STRANGER TO SOMEONE

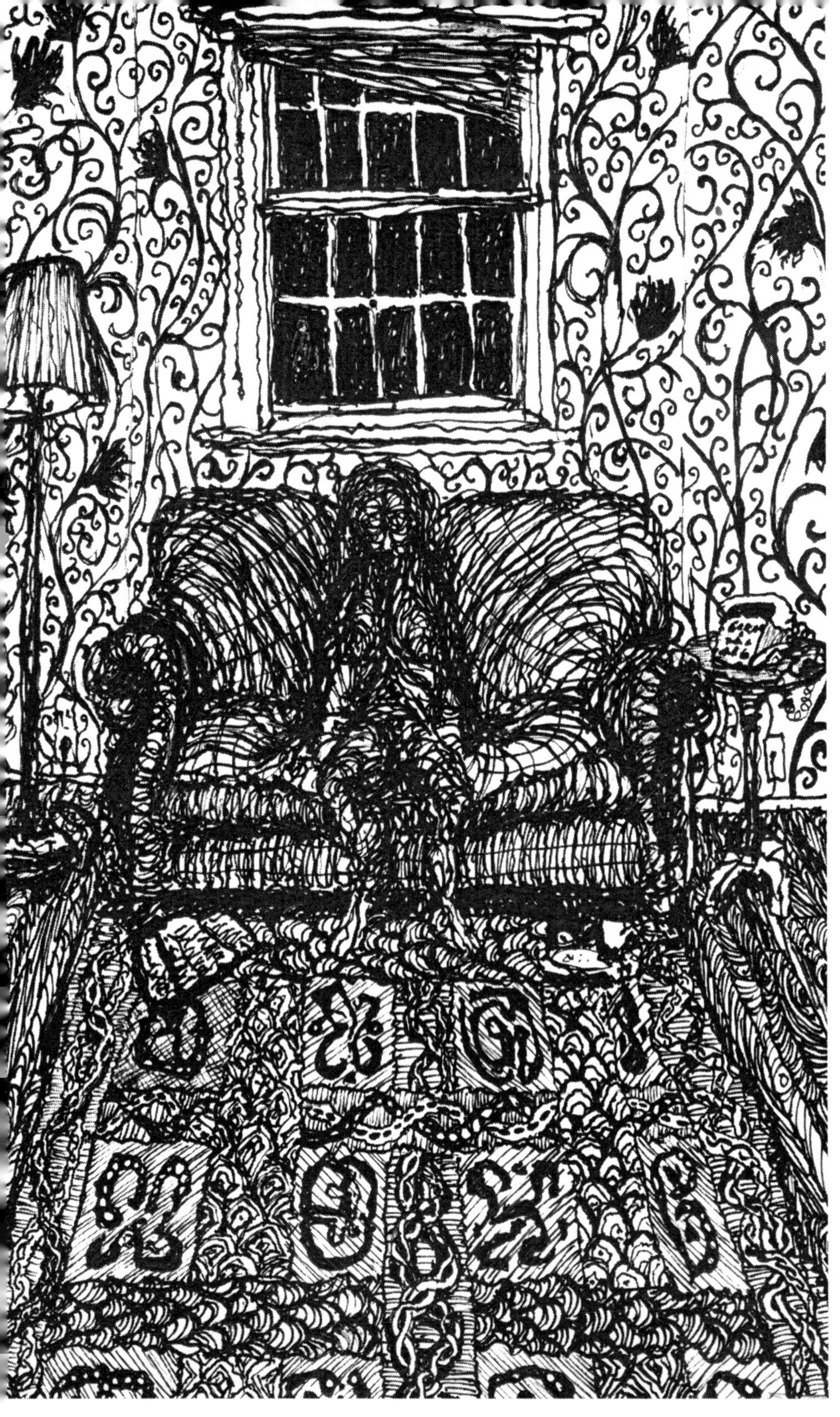

Everyone I Love is a Stranger to Someone

Ars Poetica	1
The Rules	3
Tipping Point	4
Class Of Whatever	5
Hypothetical No. 1	6
This is Called 'Great Poems'	7
Escape Artist	8
Exploded View	9
Melpomene	10
Readymade	12
Metaphor	13
<3	14
Habituation	15
Hypothetical No. 2	16
Poem to Be Found Among My Possessions Following the Occasion of My Sudden Disappearance and Analyzed for Clues as to Where I May Have Gone and Why	17
My Legacy	19
Vows	20
The Dog	21
The Electrician	22
Giraffe	23
Classical Conditioning	26
Love Poem	27
How to Be Mysterious	28
Illusionist	29
Anterograde	30
Claqueur	32
Fabulist	33
Diegesis	34
Dismissing everything you say to punish you because I love you and am afraid to lose you so must make everything into a test of commitment	35
Selfie	36
The Pillowcase	37

The More Loving One	38
Beverly Hills	39
Hurricane	40
Love Poem	42
Six Reconstructed Dreams	43
Δ	47
Abyss? What Abyss?	48
Иосиф Виссарионович Джугашвили	49
The Who's Who of Ballooning	50
Love Poem	51
:')	52
Autobiography	53
Eschatology	54
An Illustrated Guide to the Post-Apocalypse	57
About the Author	71
Acknowledgements	71

For you

Ars Poetica

A fireman puts out fires,
an artist puts out
artist's statements.
                    Hello,
my name is Annelyse. I have
chrysalized myself in the liberal arts
and now emerge, grotesque
insect, able to do nothing
but talk about everything.
I know the precise temperature
at which paper ignites.
I read a book about it.
Then I ate the book.
I have eaten so many books
by now I'm convinced
imagining and doing
are the same, which is to say
it is a miracle this poem exists
when the person who wrote it
no longer does. I read
in the book of miracles
how sometimes some residue
transfers from one encounter
to the next, one quality shared
between poetry and pinkeye.
Originally this poem was called
'Are You Serious?' and the body
was just the word 'No' like five
hundred times, but it was secretly
a rough draft, an incoherent wind
split like an infinitive
down its hideous center. I'm pretty sure
everything is a rough draft
but I've also been told I have
commitment issues but I've also

been told not to stare at the sun
and thought fuck it, why stare at anything
that doesn't blind you?, which is why
I am a poet but also why
I wear glasses. That's a nice detail.
It's easy to imagine. But 451º –
how can you imagine that?
Other facts I cannot picture in my mind:
I've been told the Earth is falling into the sun.
I've been told I'm a quick learner.
I've never stopped anything becoming ash.

The Rules

The spiral on a spiral notebook's sharp enough
to pop a water-wing. When the nurse unwound it my whole life
fell out of order. Is it such a crime to cry in a swimming pool?
Do I have to wear this bracelet? Once you're crazy
anything you do's crazy. One time I asked a blind woman

what she saw. I was six. Was that crazy? *What's behind you?*
she said. I don't know. *Exactly.* In summer camp
before I knew what deaf meant I yelled at a boy
for capturing the wrong flag. I couldn't understand why
the grownups kept saying *he's death, he's death.*

Tipping Point

Of all colors, red
has the longest wavelength
which is how blue
whales communicate at such a distance.
Street-lamps light even empty
sidewalks, sunlight's
squandered in space – no matter
the amplitude, there's a lot of waste.
Pulse is a form of
turbulence: you survive
by adapting unless you adapt
too well – then your environment
changes and you're stuck
with that one sweater
that's cute but doesn't go with anything.
Red noise, they call it.
Touch on anything's resonant
frequency, it'll shatter.
A list of possible sources
of collapse: instability,
oscillation, non-linearity, I know a great bar
down the block, there's someone
I want you to meet.

Class of Whatever

I can't recall what I did the night
I skipped out on my high school
prom. I'd already cut off my hair, eaten
an entire box of Froot Loops.

I had already invented the Anomie,
a kind of full-body flailing. You can do it
to any beat, and you may enhance
the effect of this flailing by imagining

a) your entire body is composed
of fire &/or b) the floor is wet
cement &/or c) you have married someone
whose name you cannot pronounce.

Nothing caught on. I kept reading
about the Situationists but all my friends
were already just accumulations of images.
I made my bonfire. I slept in it.

There was a teacher who told me that learning
is what's left after the facts are gone
and that's the only thing he said
I still remember.

Hypothetical No. 1

What if eyes were like teeth
so that around puberty your baby eyes would loosen and fall out
– you'd place them beneath
your pillow and wake damp between your legs with a silver dollar
under your tongue – displaced
by the grownup eyes buried all along in your eye sockets, like tulip
bulbs, only grownup eyes
were duller (there are no second chances, even in fantasy, especially in
fantasy) and more diffuse
than baby eyes, so you squandered your adolescence lamenting
your mutilated vision
finally opting for the surgery that could restore your baby eyesight
even knowing the risk
you might be left utterly blind, having decided it would be better
to see nothing than to see
everything but the brilliance you once took for granted (as you came to me
with flowers on your tongue
to see how many colors I could taste) – what would you do with me
then, with my factory
of regrets and my stupid objects, obstinately remaining what they are?

This is Called 'Great Poems'

I had a brainful of belly belly belly.
I hungered by ear to believe
I could crumple paintings and books
into the helpless furnace in my skull
and get 'Great Poems' and get
laid. The most I could get was dressed.
These sonnets are homage to old prophets
i.e. nausea. Now I owe my absurdities
to radio waves' bouncing dance – pills
are stronger than grace and singer than song!
My notebook and I are equal: demented
and all about me. I had lunch last summer
and since then I have been extinct.

Escape Artist

I've listened to this album so many times
I can't hear it anymore and I'm worried
my sex life is boring. Even our handcuffs
are cheap, the kind you can slip open
with a corkscrew and a little patience.

My drummer says he feels like he's hitting me
when he uses sticks. I can't tell if he's flirting.
I can't tell if that's okay. He's kind of a slut
but he calls himself a curator so he gets away
with it. Meanwhile I feel an obligation to mistrust

the missionary position because I had sex
in a graveyard one time and need to prove
I'm still adventurous. You have no such need.
More than once you have straddled me, gazed lovingly
into my eyes, and whispered: 'What is a shallot?'

I bought you an aluminum abacus for our
anniversary because anniversaries are dumb.
At night we get naked and you start counting
evil thoughts. Click, click, go the little beads
like tiny clocks every time you come.

Exploded View

I studied physiology because acid made me fascinated
with what could kill me. When I got my blackbird, the teacher
said: here is your magnifying glass, your tuning fork,
your one-way mirror. Lady touching holy beads, lady touching

herself in formaldehyde. On Tuesday my lab partner
said he could toggle 'acid vision' (that's what he called it) on
and off. He gave me his glasses and made the dead thing
breathe. On Wednesday he went crazy. After that it was just me

and the blackbird, styrofoam-pinned, hypochondrial sundial
misunderstanding itself into exhaustion. At home I couldn't stop
opening my wings. My parents said it was real bad luck.
The lady selling nail polish on television and the corpse wearing it

both look equally pale. The ripe blush of them
only exacerbates the effect. In class I noticed the blackbird
rotted where I touched it. I mean me. I mean I decayed
the bird. I mean none of it seemed like a coincidence.

Melpomene

Before tragedy, Melpomene was the muse
of singing. In family albums, she's the baby
swaddled in harpsilk, eyes wide and blue

bellflowers, suckling honeyed milk. Each night
above the birdcage of her crib, a mobile
orbited slow circles, propelled by the wingbeats

of nightingales tied to each axis, drifting
gentle breeze and gentler music over her.
No one spoke in her presence, so she never spoke

herself, only imitated the birdsong: a melody
for I love you, for I am hungry, for I want to be
alone. A new charm on her golden necklace

for every song she learned, until she could scarcely
lift her gentle head. When she outgrew the birdcage
she sang: build me a nest, for my hands, so long

nested from the world, are too tender to touch
anything but other hands. Sing please,
her parents commanded in song. She sang please.

Good girl. Feeding her sugarwater from a bottle
shaped like a flower, they gave her another charm.
But the night of the new nest the nightingales

sang strange and when she woke the universe
above had tilted like a lame creature and a single bird
hung lifeless, having wrapped the loyal

twine that tied it to its orbit around its loyal
neck, so that as it flew the line tautened and loyal
as always did not break. Melpomene sang I want

to be alone all morning and into night for a week.
Then two, and three by four the nightingales
dropped key. Then staggering out of her nest, scraping

her cloudbare feet on the carpet, she flung herself
to the hearth and heaved – for it was very heavy
and she very weak – her golden charm

necklace into the flames, and, filling her
bottle shaped like a flower, poured each
song molten down her tender throat.

Readymade

After so much scuttle and tinker
who can tell you what you want?
One asks for plume, receives
strangulation. Clouds
lolloping along, classified
into shapes they'll never be again.
One asks only to do a little
of the naming of things, but in the end
even asking is too much.
To the tree, a human's a bullet train.
To the train, a human's a tree.
You must crawl to walk, walk
to fall; you are entitled to fold
the pillow in half or crush
the spindlebug under your thumb
if that's what makes you happy.
I'm sorry. The porcupine's needle
quivers further into the flesh more
out of lust than revenge.
Blink once for yes, twice for no.
You will have always been good
whether you die today or whether
you have always. Dander,
dander, eiderdown. Pow!
says the bubble by the janky fist.

Metaphor

The sun is a ball of fire, counsels a voice from the catwalk.
Life is possible because we fall in its direction
and/or because we keep our distance.

Suddenly, without knowing why, everyone is aware
of breathing in. All explanation is disillusionment,
the voice is saying, all understanding incomplete.

All part of the narrative. When the heroine faints,
she is a feather. Our secret gladness is a selfish lung.
We are the audience. We're meant to hold our breath.

The lull between curtains reminds us to applaud.
Our applause reminds us of our nakedness.
That was magical, we say, to dispel the magic.

<3

I couldn't remember whether the chambers of the heart
were atria or ventricles. I looked it up. They're both.
The atrium brings the blood in, gestures to the coat
rack, pours a glass of red wine. Then out, out through
the swollen sodden gills, lub dub, all best to the wife
and kids. Missing you, there's some muscle I can't un-
tense. It's not even a vagina muscle – it's my heart.
I was thinking the heart's chambers are made of cells
which are made of chambers, but then I remembered
muscle cells are really more like those rolls of cookie dough
you slice and throw in the oven, discrete strands, maybe
string cheese would have been a better metaphor but it's
too late now, I've already made it about cookies.

If you don't like cookies then you're not paying attention.
It turns out heart cells aren't even like normal muscle cells.
They've only got one nucleus, and they spend all their lives
making sure they keep living. Under duress, their walls
thicken. I'm pretty sure someone grew them in a petri dish
and all the cells began to beat in synchrony, the tiniest
dubstep concert ever. Cardiomyocytes can grow but once
they die you're totally screwed. I didn't even want to drop
the name *cardiomyocyte*. There's a joke about monogamy in all this
somewhere. I will find it. I'll tell it to you and you'll
laugh and I'll keep tensing up my heart because if I don't
I'll die and this love poem will have been for nothing.

Habituation

You cannot feel what you expect.
Hence cannot tickle yourself. Hence
still enough in a hot bath you stop
feeling. You are not elated when he
brings home flowers. Not disappointed
when he does not. Attending only
to the surprising. The unobserved.

At first you cried astonished by
the pressure of sky on skin.
Fifteen pounds per square inch
you no longer feel or never could
because you are always pressing back.
Well-adjusted and evolved. Infants
recognize mother's voice in the womb
among all others. We can test for this.

On a quiet Thursday cutting open
melon you think of her. A train sings
outside. You mistake it for her
whistle. The five years she's been dead
you've heard it. We can test for this.
You keep slicing open your thumb.
And it hurts. It keeps hurting.

Hypothetical No. 2

Say you are a cup

the size of my hands

as full as my thirst

Poem to Be Found Among My Possessions Following the Occasion of My Sudden Disappearance and Analyzed for Clues as to Where I May Have Gone and Why

In the beginning there was the word
and before the word, silence.

Lift your hand, your thumbnail
obliterates the sun. Better to assume

the impossible jewelry of love
incomprehensible as pain.

Better to take for granted
the fishbowl's particular blue.

You are trying to find your diary.
Notice the moment before you

realize you never kept one.
Between silence and the word:

a thin silk thread, tightrope
for tiny gods, taut with attention.

You close your eyes. You walk
between awe and intimidation.

Notice anything you remember
without understanding why:

tin box rattling buttons, thumb slipped
under shirtsleeve, and so forth.

You break everything you touch. Notice
how much is achieved through mere force

of adhesion, abomination of light,
proximity, a generous loneliness.

Before the paint there was the wall.
Before the wall, wind.

Shark, papa, a shark
cries the boy, pointing to a white sail.

My Legacy

I am not really convinced I see the appeal in arranging my life in order
for a small person to take
over my uterus for nine months, like an unemployed friend
you're excited to host
at first, because he's fun to have around and accommodating him
makes you feel generous
and also wealthy, because being in a position to give means you must
have more than enough,
the way peacocks can afford their beauty's extravagant waste
because the handicap signals
fitness, like blowing a paycheck on a personal zoo would indicate
your ability to buy other, sexier
stuff – organic blueberries, vintage cars, exotic breeds of peacock
to populate your personal zoo –
but then inevitably the weekend rolls around and you
just want to sit down
and eat pizza and watch Futurama reruns, only your friend won't move
from the goddamn couch
and when you eat the pizza it somehow ends up in your friend's mouth
instead, yet it's still you
who gets fat, which is supremely unfair, especially because your friend hasn't
even tried looking for a job
and your kindness has by this point become reinforcement for his laziness
and you start wondering if he's taking
drugs or advantage of you and you're resentful and guilty for resenting him, dropping
hints that he should move out
until he finally does move out, only to occupy every other part of your house
for eighteen years straight
and order his own pizza and invite over his lame friends while your friends
offer congratulations, everyone
celebrating this ludicrous parasite, this conspicuous consumption, this shadow
who calls you mother, who
laughs just like your father, who has thoughts you have never thought and smiles
so sweetly in his sleep.

Vows

In space, no one can hear you toast the bride,
so it is easy to lie about her beauty
and your fidelity. Eventually you only mouth the words,

as you once pretended to wash your hands
by turning the tap on, then off, convinced
undisturbed and interrupted water sound the same.

Your speech closes with a simile. Later, the audio
engineers will substitute canned applause,
laughter at all the appropriate places.

The guests lift their glasses, floundering
above the banquet. Your wife points to the setting
Earth and pantomimes *Honeymoon*, which may

or may not be a question. You open your mouth,
then close it. She nods understanding as champagne arcs
from the crystal and shudders itself apart.

The Dog

Dogs need leashes. People are supposed to have
self-control. Trapped in a fire, I fluctuate
between hopping and drowning, love
and pleasure, glass of iced tea and iced tea
spoon. In your marriage, a ring –
the grand champion dog quasi-in-love
with his leash – represents sexual control
and pillowcases represent smoke.

The Electrician

They found you floating on Lake Wanaka.
Two of your legs were broken, the others
buoyed by salt and copper. Your pocket, half-

open and flapping like a gill, held a manual
for time travel in two opposite directions
without unhooking the couplers. Ink dissolves

in water, starfish swim themselves apart to grasp
a greater bamboozlement; we careen gently
toward the present tense until it's ominous

when you don't say I love you. Matisse
paints goldfish, but he's really painting
the light. I never get tired of light.

Giraffe

When a giraffe is born
it free-falls six feet from its mother's womb
straight onto its stupid head.

Welcome to the world, *Giraffa
camelopardalis*. You already look like you are
dying and your name boasts

how drunk the Romans were
when they decided you look like a camel
knocked up a leopard

in a one-night savannah
stand, except that a giraffe would not fall
six feet from a leopard

because leopards just aren't
that tall, and speaking of leopards, a lion
is 50% forecasted to eat

your face sometime this year.
Possibly the lion will be a hyena or crocodile
and probably one or more

of these animals will eat
the rest of you if and when they take your face.
You have many options in death –

in fact, far more than in life,
where things will pretty much shake out as planned:
you will fall in love with a lady

giraffe and neck a boy giraffe
to prove your devotion to her, the way Sarah Costner
made out with that blonde girl at prom

to impress her boyfriend who was so
impressed he got her pregnant so they married over summer
and divorced by finals week, except that

your chances of being alive
for long enough to marry and divorce Sarah Costner
are, according to science, slim.

Your tongue is a foot and a half
long – pretty cool, except this is only an adaptation
to get bugs out of your nose

whereas Sarah Costner has solved
this age-old quandary by not having a gigantic nose,
no offense. Your head is six

and a half feet i.e. four
and a third tongues away from your heart, which weighs
as much as two and a half

adult Maltese dogs and must pump
(your heart, not the dogs) more gallons of blood in one
minute than I drink of milk

in a year. Thinking about drinking
your blood grosses me out and makes me think of the time
my friend ate too much diner food

and coined the phrase 'drinking a milkshake
backwards,' which is gross, too, but I can't help it now, anyone
who reads this poem will think

about it now, which is the problem
with being human, which is why I envy you, giraffe,
even though your neck is both comically

long and too short to reach the ground
so that if you want to drink – water, not blood, I hope –
you have to spread your front legs

like an enormous, fleshy tripod.
I envy you even though you are so vulnerable
you can only sleep for five

minutes at a time and you
don't have any marriage rights in the United States
and your head is probably

going to have a nasty bump
from being born, whereas I went straight from the birth
canal into a giant hamburger bun

because that is how privilege
works, and I'm sorry, giraffe, but I didn't ask to be
the dominant species, the little

spoon in life's cuddle party,
the kind of animal whose body, whose very existence,
was built for sitting down.

Classical Conditioning

I didn't like the taste of alcohol before
I got drunk, and I didn't hate the word moist
until other people wouldn't shut the hell

up about how gross it sounds, which is what
I'm thinking when Dave starts in again
about how stupid the name Nickelback is

when really it's just the music that sucks
because you can make anything absurd
if you want to, like, say, the fact that words

signify and everything signed has been said
already, scrambled only to be descrambled
in one last desperate linguistic grappling hook

on consensual reality, each of us all along equally
surprised by the unshakeable logic of gratuitous
cruelty and kissing and sound whooshing faster

in water than air, which is what we're talking
about when I realize how afraid I was
to die until I met you, not to pretend

that kind of love is a new arrangement
of phonemes, but that's precisely it – that I
would gladly have anything be the last words

I ever speak – hello, I like your new haircut,
is Cup a good band name – because I'll have said it
to you who were so very almost a stranger.

Love Poem

In the story, you fall in love with a girl
on another planet. She's been dead

for years, but through your telescope
you watch her laugh, laughing too.

You wave when she, remembering
her smallness, remembers the stars.

How to Be Mysterious

There is a trick to brushing your hair
from your eyes, to leaning one-legged

against the lemon tree in your front yard
with a red ribbon around your wrist

to watch the white picket fence
sink into the white snow.

A mayfly dies the same day it's born.
A long-lived mayfly.

Nothing in this world is unlike anything else.
So many people will ask you to be

beautiful and urgent, to discover
what you cannot have and desire it.

Don't desire. Don't despair.
Rain is only rain in mid-air.

Illusionist

Dear Matthew,
Yesterday I received another of your postcards
adorned with a perfectly round tree, laminated
against the rain. *Greetings from the bottom
of the world* – they have weather stations
everywhere these days. I have forgotten
the order of seasons, traced your name in the sky
to watch the fog unwrite it. You must have seen this
coming: the letters you'd send me, the silence
I'd return.

Dear Matthew,
There is a puddle in the center of the suburbs.
It stays there all summer, never gets any smaller.
Before I outgrew it, I thought it was an ocean.
For a long time, I didn't think clouds moved at all,
just hung in the sky like portraits on a wall.

Dear Matthew,
In 1769, James Cook mapped the entire coastline
of New Zealand. The spire of the Empire State Building
was originally constructed to serve as a mooring mast
for zeppelins. Niels Bohr was once a professional
soccer player. In one of Teller's magic tricks, he cuts
the shadow of a rose with the shadow of a knife
and the real flower's petals fall to the ground.
I've watched it for years. I still don't know how it's done.

ANTEROGRADE
for H.M.

When you wake, you rewrite
in your best bedside cursive: *I am now
perfectly awake, for the first time*

like every time before. When you
blink, your hands are new hands
and you wake again, infant

flourescing into consciousness, into
shape and color and defined edge: you are
awake, you are awake, you are

walking through the plywood door
of your childhood bedroom again, still
a child again, rearranged furniture

between rearranged walls. Mural
of roses, dead fly on the windowsill.
Dead fly. You have tea, read the paper.

The war is spreading to countries
that do not exist. American women
wear nude lips. 3A. A teenage girl

in Omaha tries to kill herself with a gun
she doesn't know isn't loaded. Says
pulling the trigger is like realizing

she's locked the keys in the car.
This is devastating no matter how
  many times you read it. Many times

you read it. Many times you lock
your keys in the car. You have tea,
read the paper. Someone has filled

your sink with milky dishwater, has
already gotten the mail, has wet your
toothbrush. Mural of roses. Dead fly.

Your reflection looks older than you.
Maybe you should get more rest.
But someone has filled your bed

with newspapers. 3A. Teenage girl
in a rose-patterned dress looks like
your wife. Dead fly. Inside your mouth

feels soft and pulpy, like the end of a lollipop
stick held too long against your tongue.
You cannot remember the word *lollipop*

so think *dandelion dipped in maple sap*
but forget what the image signifies. Night falls
as a season, as a Venetian blind, as

a blind and humiliated fumble toward
some explanatory safety. If you could only stop
blinking. If you could only stop falling

asleep. It is always the same dream
you forget. In the dream, you are finally awake
and ready to receive the story of your past.

You read and reread your most important letters
but you can't remember writing them.
You can't understand what you meant.

Claqueur

After eighteen hours, the man with the camera
sliced the egg open and spilled the ostrich out.
It has to struggle to build strength, he said, but
struggling made it weak. We waited for the big
shudder to piano our rooftops, imagined drinking
the blistering fat of the yolk, fluttering to the incubator
like so many lipsticked moths to warm its ward
with our collective breath. Desperation to be undone
undid us. There is no impossible, only the unexplained.
There is no trophy for doing the right thing once.
The yolk, frankly, bored us. The ostrich was fine.
We could not rescue anything that was not already
in danger. The bird barked and barked, then began
to scream. Of course we followed its example.

Fabulist

When I got home, my bedroom was covered
in dust. The fake piano, the mantel over the fake
fireplace. The ceiling caved in while I was gone.
While I was gone they fixed it. You can still see
where it broke. I leave the opposite of a fingerprint
on whatever I touch. I have a touch lamp. I have
a fear of being misunderstood. Before the diagnosis
I told my mother I believed in magic. I didn't.
I believed it was what she needed to hear.

Diegesis

There's no natural light here, only a giant lamp
I drag across the window once a day. I'm the grip –
it's my job, passing time. I wamble over warehouse
scaffolding in my wallpaper-patterned skirt on breaks
to play house with the leading lady. God, I'm lonely
she says and I say I know. Me too. We hold hands
in her fake kitchen. The migraine surges at fake noon
and I holler turn the sun off. God, it's bright in here.
Everything I can see is contaminated with light.
The lady's at her window again, letting out her hair.
I try to climb to her, but it keeps unspooling, it's
an escalator of straw, it's the sunrise that's been shoving
my legs around to trick me into thinking I can walk.

.

DISMISSING EVERYTHING YOU SAY TO PUNISH YOU BECAUSE I LOVE YOU AND AM AFRAID TO LOSE YOU AND SO MUST MAKE EVERYTHING INTO A TEST OF COMMITMENT

like eating my way through a cathedral
full of Jello to kiss you on the mouth
or standing on your front lawn naked
humming an anthem or ode to owls

who make terrible pets according to Liza
who must 'hoot with Benny' at all hours
(Benny is the owl) and keep him inside her
home where he sweeps everything from the table

to 'make room to perch' scraping the varnish
permanently from her wardrobe in the same way
that you entered my life in lovely shambles
even though I was already this Jello-legged mouse

and you'd already kissed me like the second half
of a locket kept for years between your chest
and the world like my whole life had been
the other half and my hair smelled of peaches

which I won't pretend portends anything
but is still nice for anyone who likes peaches

Selfie

Most people are desperate and used
to sleeping alone. At 22, I consider myself
average: won't have sex

with socks on, think about death
every time I floss, quit my band before
the first practice when the name I wanted

was, according to the Internet, already taken.
Remember, anything totally unique is totally
unmemorable. To me, 'millennial' means

the box of Cheerios my father bought
in the year 2000 and keeps in his garage, deluded
into thinking it might someday be worth

something. Ditch the psychology degree
and go to law school, Cheerios, my father
is tired of your shit. Make your bed

once in a while. Stop eating in your bed.
Stop hitting yourself. When I give advice to others,
I'm really talking to me. Yes, by all means

abuse the medium. The medium's been very
very naughty. Even its safe word
makes me feel dangerous.

The Pillowcase

is printed with iridescent fish, each facing
a different direction. I bought it for you
at the Portland Goodwill our last semester

in college. Spring break we brought it camping.
I pretended I'd eaten sardines before, pretended
I liked them. I don't remember what you said

when the condom broke. Probably 'Oh, shit.'
The next day we drove into town. I took a pill
and another pill and it was over. I couldn't tell

the difference, could have told my friends
but didn't, just made lots of dead baby jokes
and went to bed in your dorm room.

You'd put painter's tape on all the edges.
With the pillowcase, it was like living in
the blueprint of an aquarium. I slept there

the night I smoked Sasha's weed and you
stayed up for hours rubbing my back, telling
fairytales so I wouldn't totally lose it.

I slept there the night I tried reading you
Haruki Murakami's *Sleep* but fell asleep. I slept
there the night after the day I lost

the bet and had to wear a lampshade on my
head and your professor said 'Nice hat.' Later I learned
she owns a lamp in the shape of a woman.

I slept there the night you said 'I think I'm
falling in love with you,' igniting a great unendurable
belongingness, like a match in a forest fire.

I burned so long so quiet you must have wondered
if I loved you back. I did, I did, I do.

The More Loving One

The year the sound came from the bottom
of the Pacific, I wouldn't undress for you
and you ate an entire window, atom by atom.

I was a knife. I was a failed romantic
gesture, but that isn't true – you couldn't be the underdog
without me. I know what you fear, love, because

I fear it too. Just between the two of us,
I was not a knife. Never expect anyone to return
what you've let them borrow.

Laura drowned herself in floodlights
singing to an auditorium full of ghosts
and you still wouldn't say you missed me.

Beverly Hills

If you can't see through the fog, maybe you should
develop an interest in fog, said T.S. Eliot's therapist.
Then the young Mr. Eliot got mired so deep in depression

he thought the fog was a cat. Low-maintenance,
doesn't come when you call, harbinger of dead pigeons,
I dunno. Who did he think he was kidding?

I'm so lonely I've entered quarantine, and even I know
fog is nothing like a cat except that both remind me
of nature and nature's a bore. In the Portland Zoo

a monkey crouches with a paper bag over its face.
Feces and ice, habitat paraphernalia. I'd hide, too, wouldn't you?
Stick my head in the hotel pool, worry about my ass

hanging out. Two Junes ago I watched a man lift a brain
out of the bloody chalice of its skull, then drove to LA
to sneak-swim in a probably lethal vodka-filled aquarium.

I was white. I fit in. I didn't even know it was a wedding.
Celebratory air at the autopsy, confetti of bone dust.
If anyone talked about Michelangelo, I didn't hear it.

Hurricane

Curse us if you will – we are already cursed
to ruin what we love and yet to love.
Everything we touch lifts to dust. Forgive us

our weakness. We have such trouble holding on,
only wanted to show you what homes are made of
by pulling them apart. We were so curious.

We didn't think of how to put them back
together. No one told us there was an order
to your grief, your stubborn acres of love

planted in something so temporary.
No one warned us how fragile your hands are.
We only wanted to help – we who lifted, we

who sank, who pulled roots of asphalt with fists
of wind to make a garden of your city. Please.
Grow. Look how little you need. We have given you

the gift of robbing you of everything
inessential. We didn't realize you never wanted
to be reminded that everything

is inessential. Forgive us. We were so
afraid. The first time we saw you, we thought
you were gods: how you pass through fields

unnoticed by the trees, the way you can leave
without leaving anything behind. There is nothing
more dangerous than something with no

destination. Forgive us our reverence. We made
skylights of your rooftops. If you had only looked up
you would have seen what became of them:

shingles chasing flocks of starlings, lawn chairs
dancing two-step with garden gnomes, orchids
in mailboxes, treehouses in the clouds.

We wanted to show you anything is possible.
Forgive us. We were so in love.
In past lives, we were mothers, and you mourned

when we promised you would outlive us.
We were firemen, and you wept when all you knew
would turn to ash turned to ash before you

were ready, because you will never be ready.
We were heart surgeons, but no one wants to hear you
can't hold on to anything without tearing it apart,

that everyone you love is a stranger to someone
who's a stranger to you, and sometimes who you love
is a stranger, too. Forgive us our strength.

We have such trouble letting go. Above the keening
branches, a smothering of clouds. Even heaven
is not perfect. Even heaven aches to hold the earth.

Love Poem

If a maple seed has fallen
probably
a maple seed has fallen
nearby

I almost never find a bird
on the ground
I almost never find a seed
in the sky

Six Reconstructed Dreams

'사람들의하는짓은알수없다'

-*Ku Sang*

1.

My hands are gloves.
My neck is a scarf.
I gesture splintered seam
unknotting my trachea
to hollow my throat.

Two fingers slipped in
a collar. Unbuttoned
at the top, little
water left in a hose.

I open my mouth
to speak, but the sound
of my voice surprises
me speechless.

2.

You are thinking lungs
do not have eyes, but
when a child is born
her lungs are closed

before she breathes
for the first time
and spends the rest
of her life blinking.

3.

In the middle of the night

I start and minutes later
the phone begins to howl
so I search for my hands
but they aren't where I
hung them on the bedpost so
the silence when you don't leave
a message is a message. I stop

asleep and in my dream
I cannot see. I look
in the mirror: I have no eyes.
Just bright receivers, buzzing
like dialtones in the dark
that cannot be dark any more
than silence can be empty.

In the morning I think I stayed
up all night hallucinating
the sound of you coming
or of you coming home.

4.

Rough draft rips the roof
from its roots like a tooth.

The Argentinian girl wants
to know what happens
when a brain receives a shock.
She pronounces it *chalk*.
He says shock is a very
general term, explains
there are two ways of being
in Spanish, speaks:
You are unfinished business.

If you want to rest in peace,
stop haunting yourself.

I apology the roof.

Estoy enferma. Motioning my unstitched skull. *Soy enferma.*

Usted es demasiadas personas,
dice él, y desaparece.

5.

I start like this because that's how dreams
are – people don't appear, they're just there.

She says I characterize things
by what they are not. I take this to mean
she is not there. I take this to mean

I have simply been writing the same poem
again and again. She offers me a wish
and says my endings are too tidy.

I want this to feel like falling
down a staircase then lying
dazed at the bottom
trying to assess
the damage.

But that's not my wish. My wish is
let me please just do one
graceful thing.

6.

By the process of elimination
I deduce the set of symbols that mean
No in a language I will never speak.

One looks like a birdbath
from a bird's-eye-view, one a half
-built fence, waiting room chair,

a human being being
swallowed by the horizon
walking away.

Δ

This time last year we were painting water.
Even then I was happy, was more than my
self. You can never get used to
the feeling of falling. When we met
I was a hell of a hollering inside, glowing
nauseous, tumbling to bioluminesce
and frankly ignoring the paint
because you will always look like something
and I have too many generic abstractions
of first scenes as mutable as the last
and goddamnit I'm a lousy painter.
In all our haphazard topographic maps, our
fatalistic whatevers, we were together.
I am with you when I'm not and I'm not
superstitious but you're still
my only parenthesis, my source.
Come February, let's go to the lake.
We'll look at the water, surprised, wondering
what water looks like.

Abyss? What Abyss?

In the movie about the aliens, San Francisco
darkens under the airship hull, a giant eye
watching itself close. There is a horizon

in every direction. A lot of crazy, sad shit happens
too fast for apprehension and all the people
in the theater start thinking maybe the theater's

the last place on Earth that's dark for good
reasons. Outside the movie, it's still too early
for hangovers and Bernal Hill still periscopes

the cochlear alleyways where amphibious traffic
echoes traffic until the whole rigmarole's
scythed over. We're doomed if the camera

doesn't linger on us, doomed if it does.
There's a crack, a crack in everything.
Well, duh. That's how the shadow gets in.

Иосиф Виссарионович Джугашвили

Her death she said about Anna Karenina
was not proved by her life. She said
in the Siberian orphanage she is remembering
hunger very well. In Riga her father was
fantastic handyman and repairing radios
even illegally in his spare time. Thank God
he was not sent to jail and heard
from his translating about the Jews.
A special dollhouse with all the furniture.
Not passenger trains but like for livestock.
He was wearing his army coat three years
after the war but always having money
for books. One day the books are in boxes
and gone to someplace. He is buying them
fur coats cheap because heavy or heavy
because cheap. He had a little flu
and then was no longer existing.
How he off took his coat entering a room.
How he took his coat unentering.
She is covering his face with a blanket
and telling her daughter to go visit
her grandmother my grandmother said.
She is drinking her breath from the faucet.
Time passes but it stays here. She is
not pointing to her heart but her throat.

The Who's Who of Ballooning

The scientist got rich off this study showing rich people
were assholes. After that he quit his job and bought

a hot air balloon. He painted it blue and white
and rich people paid him to make them high and invisible.

They hung in the clouds wondering if they were assholes.
One by one the indeterminate sky swallowed their wonder

and their wonder fell straight through it, like a body
through a ghost. Flying isn't amazing, but it's amazing to fly, but

in the end it's always some bird that gets in the way
or some guy in a lawn chair levitated by some birds.

The scientist had a promising career in standup comedy
before he blew his second special only talking in cumulus.

Love Poem

The moon wanted to be an astronaut.

She shot up to the Earth's
outer limits and went to sleep.

:')

In the wet dreaming room seventeen and a half boys
masturbate on seventeen and a half make-believe beds,
sleeping hands tied round seventeen and a half blue roses
blooming to the organ-grinder's song.
In every way, they are their sustained melodic breakdown,
unadorned emotion cast off outside our atonal
scudding. O let me dream not the logic of boats
but of rooms billowing with brackish wine,
you and me lost at sea, reed-deep in the technical journals.
We are a helpless make-believe presence deteriorating
except in alcohol. Do you want me to take off my human
myself? Sailboat, frail boat – ugly and marvelous body!
There is no such thing as a patternless universe.
There is really no such thing as a birdless place.

Autobiography

Light sterile as sound or sadness
thrums between the parted palms
of sea and sky, sky and blue tin roof
I saw and from which saw for miles
cardboard rafters and dotted ceiling tiles
to count as stars, to offer proof:
light outposts even on the moon.
We move our skin from room to room.
Essay the body, embassy threatened:
what passes must be progress or else
nothing meant, so never mentioned.
Leaves make beds of winter ground.
Sunlight, surgeon, makes its rounds.

Eschatology

I am a functional adult, more or less literally
maintaining the fuck out of my relationships.
I put my face on the cat's face yesterday
and she tried to smother me with the tiny pillow

of her paws. Can someone please make a forklift
that looks like that cat? said my housemate
but she meant a different cat so I stopped listening.
My boyfriend brought me a plastic bag of room

-temperature ham. Earlier, a can of sweetened
condensed milk. I don't even own a can opener.
I am the most helpless thing I can think of –
rattlesnake in a wheelchair, wheelchair

on ice. I just want to use the word *scaleneness*
and refer to my sex drive as a pocket and stop
justifying this bogus madness hunted
to extinction by post-inspiration French guys.

If you took away thoughts like 'I can't believe
I'm not dead,' I wouldn't have any idea who I am,
which I think says a lot about who I am
or at least says I'm not dead, which is something.

Further proof that I am not dead: a) I checked out
War and Peace from the library in December
2012 and I look at its spine every day and I still
haven't opened it once, I just keep renewing it, and

b) I've looked up the difference between metonymy
and synecdoche like nine times but I can never
keep them straight, yet I still can quote almost
all of Finding Nemo from memory.

An Illustrated Guide to the Post-Apocalypse

"What?"

- Hamlet, to the Ghost

1.

The future has an obscenely happy
ending: one day there you are
then suddenly BANG!
        3am
and you're spending the rest of eternity
eating a plate of eggs over easy
listening 102.1, incandescent with fever—
        You look at me and I begin to shine
        Just like the sun when it tells the moon you're mine
—sing along, you lovesick vampire—
        And I'm crazy 'bout ya, baby, can't you see
        So don't you dare go ahead and die on me

2.

Fifteen people have lived and died
for every one still alive
and that's just the pre-apocalypse—my god!
We're the protagonists of our own stories
trapped in the basement of our lives!
I will wipe the yolk from your chin
and paint our faces green
so when the aliens find us
they'll nod *Keep up the good work*
instead of kidnapping us for their human milking machine—
that is how much I love you.

3.

A conductor, an undercover cop,
and a functional adult
walk into a bar. Happy birthday—
let's get wasted and watch late-night television!
Close your eyes and make a wish!
(blowjobs blowjobs blowjobs)
Now back to our scheduled programming—
but first
our weekly weather forecast: there will be girls!
(girls girls girls girls)

4.

It was winter for years. I had your voice-
mails on repeat like digital jukeboxes
eating all my quarters in new AAAs.
Did you know three people were crushed
to death by vending machines in 1988?
I bet too many people couldn't eat just one
and one and one and I can't blame them—
you are my favorite song, all clattering
cages, shattering bulbs, dead skin cells
grind-dancing dead skin cells
like tinder on kindling, keeping me warm.

5.

Sometimes I imagine you've died
instead of just moving to Chicago
and how impossible it would be
to replace you. When the world ends
there will be no cars or textiles or houses
that aren't blueprinted in Kid Pix, no food that isn't Easy
Mac looted from abandoned supermarkets.
I love you like a felony conviction. I love you
because you weigh probably 600 pounds
less than a vending machine
which is one less way for you to kill me.
Take off my skin before the atom bomb, pronounce
my name like identity theft, fill your lungs
with ghost-muffled sirens to bless
the brittle refuge of my ankles.
I love you cosmic anonymity
I love you organized a little
out of entropy I love you
pale blue dot in the red shift I love.

6.

Welcome to continued existence
in the face of nothingness, this electron-
aimless search for a heart that open
-swings like a gate, and that's not
all—you've got to knock
and see if someone is home
and if they are
do they want to buy a subscription
to *US Weekly?*

Long odds, yeah, but you've got to
do it—that's life.
You can't touch the world
without being touched back,
not even after the world ends.
Every breath is still shameless seduction,
every moment the latest vital scene—
so applause my hands, you — you accident of flesh—
We are not victims of life!
We are survivors of death.

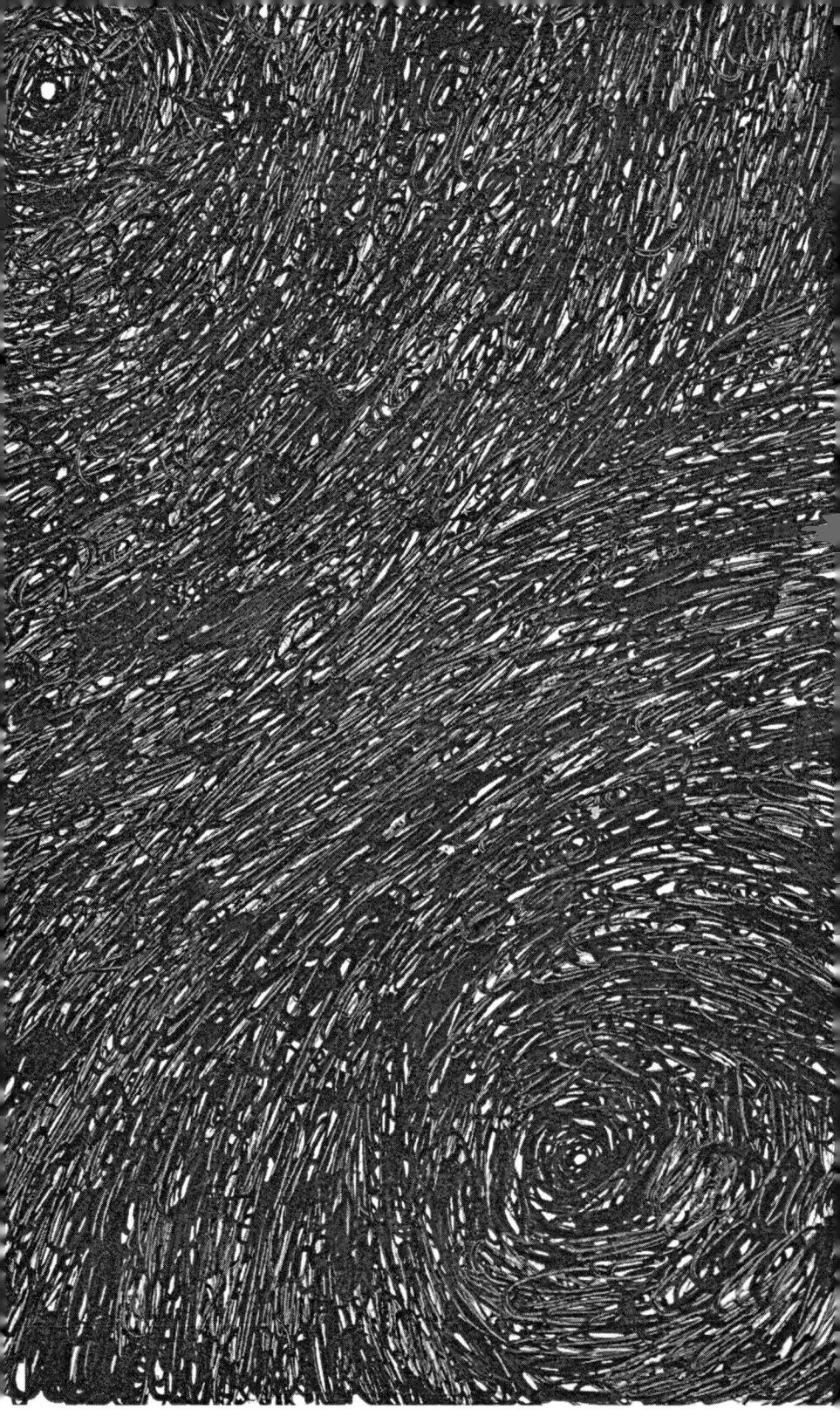

About the Author

Annelyse Gelman is a California Arts Scholar, the inaugural poet-in-residence at UCSD's Brain Observatory, and recipient of the 2013 Mary Barnard Academy of American Poets Prize and the 2013 Lavinia Winter Fellowship. She divides her time between the United States and New Zealand. Find her at www.annelysegelman.com.

Acknowledgements

Thank you to the editors and staff of the following journals, where many of the poems in this book first appeared: *Hobart* (Eschatology, Escape Artist); *Swarm* (<3); The Destroyer and *Atticus Review* (Giraffe); *Rufous City Review* (This is Called 'Great Poems'); *Former People* (The Who's Who of Ballooning, The Electrician); *The Economy* (Tipping Point); *Nailed Magazine* (Illusionist, Six Reconstructed Dreams, Melpomene, Hypothetical No. 2, Poem to Be Found Among My Possessions and Analyzed for Clues as to Where I May Have Gone and Why); *MARY* (Hurricane); and *Australian Book Review* (Class of Whatever).

Thank you to Jacopo Annesse and the UCSD Brain Observatory, the Winter family and New Pacific Studio, and Michael Knutson and the board of the Kaspar T. Locher Scholarship.

Thank you to Brian Ellis, Eliana Gray, Jae Choi, Jodie Dalgleish, Sabrina Swerdloff, and Samiya Bashir for your criticism, to Auden Lincoln-Vogel for your vision, and to my past, current, and future friends and family for your support.

If You Liked Annelyse Gelman, Annelyse Gelman likes . . .

Over the Anvil We Stretch
Anis Mojgani

Uncontrolled Experiments in Freedom
Brian Ellis

Spiking the Sucker Punch
Robbie Q Telfer

Everything is Everything
Cristin O'Keefe Aptowicz

Slow Dance With Sasquatch
Jeremy Radin

Write Bloody Publishing distributes and promotes great books of fiction, poetry, and art every year. We are an independent press dedicated to quality literature and book design, with an office in Austin, TX.

Our employees are authors and artists, so we call ourselves a family. Our design team comes from all over America: modern painters, photographers, and rock album designers create book covers we're proud to be judged by.

We publish and promote 8 to 12 tour-savvy authors per year. We are grass-roots, D.I.Y., bootstrap believers. Pull up a good book and join the family. Support independent authors, artists, and presses.

**Want to know more about Write Bloody books, authors, and events?
Join our mailing list at**

www.writebloody.com

WRITE BLOODY BOOKS

After the Witch Hunt — Megan Falley

Aim for the Head, Zombie Anthology — Rob Sturma, Editor

Amulet — Jason Bayani

Any Psalm You Want — Khary Jackson

Birthday Girl with Possum — Brendan Constantine

The Bones Below — Sierra DeMulder

Born in the Year of the Butterfly Knife — Derrick C. Brown

Bring Down the Chandeliers — Tara Hardy

Ceremony for the Choking Ghost — Karen Finneyfrock

Courage: Daring Poems for Gutsy Girls — Karen Finneyfrock, Mindy Nettifee & Rachel McKibbens, Editors

Dear Future Boyfriend — Cristin O'Keefe Aptowicz

Dive: The Life and Fight of Reba Tutt — Hannah Safren

Drunks and Other Poems of Recovery — Jack McCarthy

The Elephant Engine High Dive Revival anthology

Everything Is Everything — Cristin O'Keefe Aptowicz

The Feather Room — Anis Mojgani

Gentleman Practice — Buddy Wakefield

Glitter in the Blood: A Guide to Braver Writing — Mindy Nettifee

Good Grief — Stevie Edwards

The Good Things About America — Derrick Brown and Kevin Staniec, Editors

Hot Teen Slut — Cristin O'Keefe Aptowicz

I Love Science! — Shanny Jean Maney

I Love You is Back — Derrick C. Brown

The Importance of Being Ernest — Ernest Cline

In Search of Midnight — Mike McGee

The Incredible Sestina Anthology — Daniel Nester, Editor

Junkyard Ghost Revival anthology

Kissing Oscar Wilde — Jade Sylvan

The Last Time as We Are — Taylor Mali
Learn Then Burn — Tim Stafford and Derrick C. Brown, Editors
Learn Then Burn Teacher's Manual — Tim Stafford and Molly Meacham, Editors
Live For A Living — Buddy Wakefield
Love in a Time of Robot Apocalypse — David Perez
The Madness Vase — Andrea Gibson
The New Clean — Jon Sands
New Shoes On A Dead Horse — Sierra DeMulder
No Matter the Wreckage — Sarah Kay
Oh, Terrible Youth — Cristin O'Keefe Aptowicz
The Oregon Trail Is the Oregon Trail — Gregory Sherl
Over the Anvil We Stretch — Anis Mojgani
Pole Dancing to Gospel Hymns — Andrea Gibson
Racing Hummingbirds — Jeanann Verlee
Rise of the Trust Fall — Mindy Nettifee
Scandalabra — Derrick C. Brown
Slow Dance With Sasquatch — Jeremy Radin
The Smell of Good Mud — Lauren Zuniga
Songs from Under the River — Anis Mojgani
Spiking the Sucker Punch — Robbie Q. Telfer
Strange Light — Derrick C. Brown
These Are The Breaks — Idris Goodwin
Time Bomb Snooze Alarm — Bucky Sinister
The Undisputed Greatest Writer of All Time — Beau Sia
What Learning Leaves — Taylor Mali
What the Night Demands — Miles Walser
Working Class Represent — Cristin O'Keefe Aptowicz
Write About An Empty Birdcage — Elaina Ellis
Yarmulkes & Fitted Caps — Aaron Levy Samuels
The Year of No Mistakes — Cristin O'Keefe Aptowicz
Yesterday Won't Goodbye — Brian S. Ellis

CPSIA information can be obtained at www.ICGtesting.com
Printed in the USA
BVOW05s2029140414

350364BV00002B/9/P